School of Prayer, Prophecy and *"Greater things"*

TRAINING & ACTIVATION MANUAL

SPIRITUAL GIFTS

Prophecy & Prophetic Ministry

Servant Robin

TRAINING & ACTIVATION MANUAL; Course 2: PROPHECY & PROPHETIC EVANGELISM

Copyright © 2012 Robin Jegede-Brimson
No part of this book may be reproduced or transmitted in any form or by any means, electronic, mechanical, photocopying and recording or by any information storage and retrieval system without written permission from the author.

All scripture quotations, unless otherwise indicated, are taken from the Holy Bible, New International Version®, NIV®. Copyright ©1973, 1978, 1984, 2011 by Biblica, Inc.™ Used by permission of Zondervan. All rights reserved worldwide. www.zondervan.com. The "NIV" and "New International Version" are trademarks registered in the United States Patent and Trademark Office by Biblica, Inc.™

"Scripture quotations taken from the Amplified® Bible, Copyright © 1954, 1958, 1962, 1964, 1965, 1987 by The Lockman Foundation. Used by permission." (www.Lockman.org)

Published by SERVANT BOOKS   www.servantministries.co.uk   2021 edition

AFRICA
Henry Hamilton
Servant Ministries Nigeria
U.I.P.O. Box 22974, Ibadan, Nigeria.
Tel +234 080 3368 1552.
E–mail: hamiltonh78@hotmail.com

EUROPE
Robin Jegede-Brimson
Servant Ministries
7, Belton Close, Whitstable, Kent
CT5 4LG, UK
Tel +44 0787 202 4364
E–mail: GodsOyster@aol.com

Cover design by
BARLT GRAPHICS PRINTS, NIG.
+234(0) 70 3822 8234
topekanbi@yahoo.com

To David, Paul, Prince and Deborah – having you has enriched me beyond my wildest dreams

Contents

- INTRODUCTION ... 7
  - SECTION A BASIC PROPHETIC EQUIPPING (18 hours) ... 9
  - LESSON 1: DEFINITIONS ... 11
  - LESSON 2: THE BAPTISM OF THE HOLY SPIRIT & THE REVELATORY GIFTS ... 13
  - LESSON 3: HOW TO RECEIVE & "WEIGH" A PROPHETIC WORD ... 15
  - LESSON 4: HOW TO PROPHESY ... 17
  - LESSON 5 CORE VALUES ... 21
  - LESSON 6: BREAK OUT GROUP GUIDELINES & LEADERS NOTES ... 23
  - LESSON 7: "SOAKING" AND BEING "DRUNK IN THE SPIRIT" ... 25
  - LESSON 8: ACTIVATIONS INTO THE SCREEN ON YOUR MIND, WORDS OF KNOWLEDGE, PROPHECY, TRAVELLING IN THE SPIRIT, DISCERNING OF SPIRITS AND MORE ... 27
  - SECTION B GROWING INTO PROPHETIC MINISTRY (9 hours) ... 30
  - LESSON 9: GROWING IN PROPHETIC FLOW ... 32
  - LESSON 10: MORE GUIDELINES FOR UNDERSTANDING & GIVING PROPHECY ... 35
  - LESSON 11: MORE ON PROPHETIC FLOW & PROTOCOLS ... 39
  - LESSON 12: CONDITIONAL & UNCONDITIONAL PROPHECY, PLUMBLINES ... 42
  - LESSON 13: THE CALLING TO PROPHETIC MINISTRY ... 44
  - SECTION C SHADES OF PROPHETIC MINISTRY (8 hours) ... 46
  - LESSON 14: DISCERNING OF SPIRITS, DREAMS & VISIONS ... 48
  - LESSON 15: PROPHETIC ACTIONS, WALKS & DRIVES & PROCLAMATIONS ... 52
  - LESSON 16: PROPHETIC EVANGELISM, TREASURE HUNTS ... 54
  - LESSON 17: PROPHETIC EVANGELISM (2) Practicals, Tips & Pointers ... 58
  - LESSON 18: PROPHETIC DEPARTMENTS ... 62
  - SECTION D THE OFFICE OF A PROPHET (5 hours) ... 63
  - LESSON 19: THE PREPARATION OF A PROPHET ... 65
  - LESSON 20: THE MINISTRY OF A PROPHET ... 77
- IPAA DEFINITION AND CRITERIA OF A PROPHET ... 77
  - LESSON 21: PROPHETIC APPOINTMENTS ... 82
  - 12 TESTS & INDICATORS OF PROPHETIC OFFICE ... 84
- ABOUT THE AUTHOR ... **Error! Bookmark not defined.**

This is a 40-hour course comprising of 30 hours of instruction interspersed with 10 hours of activations, prayer and worship. This could be done from anything from 8 weeks to 18 months depending on how regularly meetings are held.

INTRODUCTION

In Course 1: "Prayer", we looked at 30 different types of prayer and our reliance on The HOLY SPIRIT in order to effectively use them in our walk with GOD. We also saw how The HOLY SPIRIT blesses us with various gifts (tongues, interpretation of tongues, identificational repentance, deep groans of intercession etc) to help us pray certain prayer forms that are beyond our natural ability.

Our study of prayer and operating in the gifts that The HOLY SPIRIT has given us now continues with the many forms that prophetic gifting take. Certain aspects that were taught in Course 1 will be useful in pressing in to this course, so avail yourself of the opportunity to get a copy if you can.

So, why study PROPHECY & the functions of the prophetic office?

THE PROPHETIC LEADS THE CALL OF THE CHURCH TO PRAYER & ACTION
1Corinthians 14:8; Acts 11:27-30
A major function of the prophetic is to sound a trumpet that mobilises the church to PRAYER. When prophets sound the trumpet of alarm it is a rallying call to pray or action. Some of this may be to petitioning governmental bodies and leaders of nations. It is sounding an alarm.

PROPHECY IS A GIFT FOR ALL
Joel 2:28,29: Numbers 11:29; 1Corinthians 14:31; 1Sam 10:9,10; Lk 1:39-46;1:67
At the birth of the church on the day of Pentecost, Peter stood up and preached from a promise that all sons and daughters will one day prophesy. Moses, the deliverer of the children of Israel desired that all would prophesy. Paul the apostle also asked all who were in the church at Corinth to earnestly desire to prophesy, categorically saying that all could.

THE PROPHETIC LEADS THE SAINTS INTO ENCOUNTERS WITH THE UNSAVED
1Corinthians 14:24,25; John 4; Acts 8:26-29; 11:4,12,15; 16;9,10
The secrets of men hearts are revealed in prophetic words. Through prophetic words The Church is led into encounters with those prepared beforehand by The LORD.

THE PROPHETIC WARNS THE CHURCH OF THINGS TO COME & RELEASES OTHER MINISTRIES
Acts 11:27-30;21:10,11; 13:1-4
The prophetic gives us eyes to see and ears to hear.
And as we will see further in this study (page 45) the prophetic is also charged with managing the flow of The SPIRIT in the setting up of prophetic protocols, commissioning ministries, visions and directions and the setting up of worship altars.

This manual is in four sections covering; -
A) The basics of prophecy
B) Developing into prophetic ministry
C) Fields of prophetic
D) The Ministry Office of a Prophet

It could be taken as a 40-hour course comprising of 30 hours of instruction interspersed with 10 hours of activations, prayer and worship. This could be done from anything from 8 weeks to 18 months depending on how regularly meetings are held.

Love in CHRIST

Robin Jegede-Brimson
October 2018

SECTION A
BASIC PROPHETIC EQUIPPING
(18 hours)

Section introduction

Prophetic equipping opens the door to all the nine gifts of the spirit mentioned by Paul, the apostle in 1Corinthians 12. This is all for believers whatever your primary calling may be and provides a foundation for effective spiritual growth. A percentage of those who undergo this equipping will find themselves called to either prophetic ministry or the office of a prophet. A portion of those so equipped will also find that they achieve a proficiency in the power gifts (healings, miracles and faith) leading them into the calling of an evangelist or apostolic ministry or the office of an apostle. It is our role to be equipped in the rudiments of the revelatory gifts and to obey Paul in earnestly seeking to prophecy and to operate in the "best gifts". The particular "administration" or office we find ourselves in ultimately depends on the calling of GOD into that sphere.

Personal notes

_____

_____

_____

LESSON 1: DEFINITIONS

a. PROPHESY/PROPHECY

1Corinthians 12: 4-11, 14:3, 31; Acts 19:6; Joel 2:28; Acts 2:1-18;

The simple gift of prophecy is to encourage and edify. It is an affirmation of The FATHER's love, sovereignty and protection. Everyone is called and can operate in this gift. We are called to desire it. This gift is given by the will and operation of The HOLY SPIRIT.

It is GOD's will for every believer to prophesy. This is in fulfilment of Joel's prophecy quoted by Peter:-
"I will pour out my Spirit on all people. Your sons and daughters will prophesy, your old men will dream dreams, your young men will see visions. Even on my servants, both men and women, I will pour out my Spirit in those days. (Joel 2:28)

Prophecy can be defined as: -

- A word or act originating from the HOLY SPIRIT that encourages, builds up and comforts.

- A word or act that reveals or releases the heart and mind of GOD into a particular context or situation.

- Seeing or perceiving in the spiritual realm (combined with 'seer gift' or 'discerning of spirits') *(Numbers 12:6)*

We get these basic definitions from *1Corinthians 14:3 "The one who prophesies speaks to people for their strengthening, encouraging and comfort"*

'Prophecy is supernatural utterance in a known tongue. The Hebrew meaning of the phrase, "to prophesy" is to flow forth. It also carries with it the thought: to bubble forth like a fountain, to let drop, to lift up, to tumble forth, and to spring forth. The Greek word that is translated "prophesy" means to speak to one another. So "prophesy" can mean to speak for GOD or be his spokesperson'
'The HOLY SPIRIT and His Gifts' by Kenneth Hagin (pg 139)

The gift of prophecy is often a mix of both "now words" (word of knowledge) as well as 'future-telling' - predicting future events (prophecy).

When a fact or aspect is revealed in prophecy it is the 'Word of Knowledge' which is in operation in conjunction with prophecy. This piece of knowledge could be about something from the past or the present.

Revelation about the future e.g. "You will find a colt tied". is an operation of the gift of prophecy.

A "word of wisdom" is an instruction emanating from The SPIRIT of GOD which when followed and carried out in faith triggers and releases the supernatural power of GOD. This can result in a healing, a flow of resources or any other type of miracle. Examples are when Elijah said to cast a stick into the water, told Naaman to bathe in the River Jordan, or when JESUS told Peter to fish for a coin. It is the supernatural wisdom and direction of GOD to bring solutions in life.

This is different from walking in wisdom or acquiring general wisdom from the SPIRIT of GOD. Spiritual gifts by definition are by the prompting of The HOLY SPIRIT, we do not walk in them 24/7 but only as He wills.

The two revelatory gifts of word of knowledge and word of wisdom are usually aspects of the gift of prophecy.

A fourth revelatory gift is called "the discerning of spirits". This is seeing in the realm of the spirit. This seeing causes us to be able to interact with and affect things from the spirit realm. This gift can work as a sense of seeing like in a vision, or a sense of smell where one discerns a smell in the spiritual realm.

b. PROPHET

Ephesians 4:9-11; 1Timothy 3:1;

This is someone who is called to the ministry and office of a prophet. While it is good to desire and aspire to leadership, the selection of what 5-fold ministry office we occupy is left to the discretion of The LORD JESUS. See

c. To PROPHESY

Ezekiel 37; 1Kings 13:1-6; Ezra 6:14; Acts 19:6; Jonah 3:1-4

This can refer to the act of: -

    a. Bringing a word of encouragement from The LORD to an individual or a gathering

    b. Bringing a revelatory word, which contains extra stuff beyond just encouragement.

    c. Releasing a destructive word from The LORD

    d. Releasing a creative word; forth-telling, declaring & calling things into existence

    e. Giving a word of warning

NOTES

LESSON 2: THE BAPTISM OF THE HOLY SPIRIT & THE REVELATORY GIFTS

Acts 19:6, 1Corinth 12:10, and 1Samuel 10:6; 1Corinth 14:31; 1Corinth 12:31, 14:39.

By the revelatory gifts we mean the gifts which reveal something (Prophecy, words of knowledge and discerning of spirits)

On one of the occasions in Acts of the Apostles when the baptism of the HOLY SPIRIT was received, in addition to speaking in tongues they also prophesied right away. Earlier on in the birthing of The Church on the day of Pentecost in second chapter of Acts Peter explained the phenomenon of speaking in tongues by quoting from Joel 2:28. Here however Joel spoke of dreams, vision & prophecy as products of The SPIRIT of GOD being poured out. So, if we camp at merely praying in tongues, we are short changing ourselves.

We've seen that as people are baptised in The Spirit they can also receive the gift of prophecy. This gift is open to all and Paul encourages us all to seek for it.

John 10:27 "My sheep hear My voice, and I know them, and they follow Me."

We can all learn how to hear HIS Voice and then to speak out what we hear

1 Corinthians 14:31 Not all are called to be a prophet to the church but all CAN prophesy. *"Can"* (Greek *dunasthe*) means to be intrinsically or absolutely able — you have the power!)

The ability to prophesy can come on one of four levels:

1. A spirit of prophecy as in 1Sam 10 & 19. The atmosphere was so thick everyone could!

2. A gift of simple prophecy — every believer can operate at this level

3. Prophetic ministry. A level of proficiency and an understanding of the ins and outs of prophesying

4. Prophetic office. Mature and called by CHRIST into this office

The prophetic grace can be released in numerous ways e.g.

1. In prophesying
2. In singing a new song
3. In creative dance or theatre
4. In waving flags and banners
5. In prophetic art
6. In prophetic outreach

LESSON 3: HOW TO RECEIVE & "WEIGH" A PROPHETIC WORD

Before we turn the page and begin to activate into the revelatory gifts, we want to teach HOW TO HANDLE THEM! Prophecy, visions, "thus says The LORD" and such stuff can build as well as wreck lives. So, like we would with fireworks or a nail gun which are all great, it is good to first learn the pros and cons. This lesson is about keeping prophecy safe.

This is in accordance with the scriptures

"Test all things" (1Thess 5:21) "Let the others weigh" (1Corinthians 14:29)

1. Are you unsure of or intimidated by, the person wanting to share a word with you? Ask them nicely to call a friend or leader alongside or just say, *"Thanks but no thanks!"* If they might need one, offer a mint – be comfortable!

2. Reach for a pen and paper or your "record" function on your mobile - great riches need to be preserved well!

3. Be open, be sure, you are free to ask for clarification, to interject or to ask them to slow down, rewind or stop! It is your word!

4. If you feel imposed upon or the word does not witness with where you are DO NOT receive the word. Say thank you and ask to move on. If you feel neutral about the word, then simply store the word away (on a shelf).
Please note: Prophetic words are not the avenue for correction. Correction comes from those you have given permission to out of trust and developing relationship

5. Tune in on 3 levels – the revelation (purest form), the interpretation (subjective) the application (left to you really). Be gracious - take the meat – spit out the bones (there will almost always be a bit of a mix)

6. All prophetic words have a moral imperative to them – *e.g. "because . . . "* 1Sam 15:23; 2Chron 15:2; 16:7-9; 1Samuel 2:30

7. Prophetic declarations might also demand an obligation to a life of prayer and closeness to The HOLY SPIRIT *1Tim 1:18.19; James 5:17; Luke 2:25*

8. Testing a directional prophetic word?
    a. Is it line with GOD's written word?
    b. Is it in accordance with the spirit of the Bible?
    c. Does it reflect the Father Heart of GOD? Do we hear and perceive GOD in this?
    d. A word may be accurate but from a wrong spirit (extreme cases) eg Acts 16:16-18
    e. Is there a wrong motive behind it?
    f. Is it in any way controlling? Does it subjugate someone else's will?
    g. How does it 'sit' with you?

9. Sometimes a word is speaking in, creating something that is not there yet. Especially if you sense an anointing (a release of power, an ummphh!) in it. In which case respond with an "Amen!" ie "so be it", "I agree!"

10. Thank the person who prophesied over you. They took a risk and often needed to step out of their comfort zone. Be gracious even if aspects don't match where you are right now. Find the aspect that spoke to you and hold it close.

LESSON 4: HOW TO PROPHESY

There are four components to every prophetic word

1. The revelation
   What you rec'd from The HOLY SPIRIT. This could be in one of various forms through any of your senses – a picture, a memory, an emotion, a physical sensation and so forth

   NOTES

2. The interpretation
   This is answering the question, "So what does this mean? What scriptural truth or reality does GOD wish to convey through this?"

   NOTES

3. The application
   Following on from one or more interpretations, how do I believe this is to be applied to the person I am prophesying to?

   NOTES

4. The delivery
   What tone of voice and manner of expression is appropriate for communicating this message. What language should I use? "I believe GOD is saying…" or "The LORD showed me…" etc. the best delivery comes from grasping the heart of GOD and with experience.

   NOTES

PRAYER: "Precious HOLY SPIRIT I submit my mind, will and emotions to You"
(Hebrews 4:12)

This is a great prayer to pray each time we go to seek GOD to be used as His mouthpiece to others. We don't want our own opinion getting in the way!

So, in a sentence, (which we will break down as we go) to prophecy is to ….

Prepare your heart . . . to receive revelation, then lean into GOD to lead you to the right interpretation; offer your revelation in love and humility, as you wait (together) for the right application - umpired by peace in your heart.

- A) ***Prepare your heart . .***

    Prophesy out of love – this is the test for a <u>true</u> prophetic word! (1Corinthians 13)

    Take off from 1Corinthians 14:3 "The one who prophesies speaks to people for their strengthening, encouraging and comfort"

    If unsure, rehearse it in your mind to yourself - does it inspire hope, lifting, courage? Ask HOLY SPIRIT for wisdom on how to phrase what He is communicating to you - would you like to receive this word yourself? Are you communicating it in the right disposition?

- B) ***. . to receive revelation*** (1 minute waiting on GOD for a word)

    This could come either through a model you are comfortable with: –

1) Using analogies - ask GOD to show you -
    a. A plant or an animal that depicts certain notable characteristics about the person you are ministering to
    b. A Bible character that comes to mind
    c. A Bible passage (2Tim 3:16)
    d. Something that the person you are prophesying over is wearing <u>that strikes you</u>
    e. A mode of transport
    f. A popular play or movie
    g. A colour
    h. A number
    i. A date

2) Or asking for revelation through one of your spiritual senses
    a. Something that flashes across your mind / <u>imagination</u> (don't second guess!) (Eph 1:17-19)
    b. A phrase that comes to your heart
    c. A picture you see (you can draw it) - be open for it to become a movie! (Jeremiah 1:11-13)

3) Or a -

a. Memory from the past (Mark 8:18); The word of testimony releases the same power as in the event you remember (Ps 78:1-11)

b. Word of knowledge (a feeling, an "inner knowing", a pain in your body, an emotion) As the revelatory aspect of your prophetic word comes, prepare to flow with it, <u>trusting GOD</u> for more insight as you begin to speak.

c. ***. . lean on GOD to lead you to the right interpretation. . .*** At this stage in your prophetic journey feel very much at ease with sharing what you have been given to 'know' - it's ok to not be able to work it all out.

d. ***. .then <u>offer</u> your revelation in love and humility*** (1-2 minutes each)

e.g. "I saw _____ does this mean anything to you?" "I feel that GOD may be saying . . ."
we are called to serve not impose or coerce people into receiving our prophecy.

C) ***. . as you wait (together) for the right application - umpired by peace in your heart.***
Let the recipient give feedback (1 minute) e.g. "Wow yes, this meant so much to me!" "Thank you I can relate to this and this but I'm not sure about this bit"

D) If in a group setting let the group leader (or someone appointed) offer prayer for the recipient based on the feedback.

LESSON 5 CORE VALUES

1. Motivation –
    a. GOOD - love, encouragement
    b. POOR – visibility, having "something to say"
2. Look for treasure – eg simon – peter
3. Convict of the glory they are falling short of . .
4. 1Corinthinas 14:24-25 fall down and worship (*repent* – change of mind or viewpoint)
5. Lean on redemptive grace - Romans 8:28. Seek for the redemptive purpose on all prophecies, particularly the difficult ones
6. Include young people
7. We are being equipped to take this to the world so as much as possible leave off religious stuff, clichés, prayer forms etc (preserve the freshness of The HOLY SPIRIT and guard against religion)
8. Calling people up higher, into their destiny in God; Bring hope, release hope
9. Safeguarding vulnerability. Don't play on peoples weaknesses
10. Personal prophecy – yes; private prophecy – no.
11. Directional words? Put loads of protective bubble wrap around it! Offer in loads of humility and be vulnerable and open . . also input according to relationship
12. Nobody gets it 100% of the time all the time. This is humility, this is openness to receiving correction from others. This is growth.

BEST PRACTISE

1. Is the need of the person best served by a reminder of biblical principles? The bible shares the principles – the strategy; prophecy serves the tactics.

2. A word to a young person? Let their guardian or parent be with you

3. Don't prophecy out of what you know or a personal desire to bring correction without clarifying this and making a distinction between what you know and what you are sensing GOD is wanting to say into this e.g "I am aware that you are thinking of moving home and I feel GOD is saying _____ "

LESSON 6: BREAK OUT GROUP GUIDELINES & LEADERS NOTES

For use in group sessions with four or five in a group over an hour practising and learning together as we grow in confidence

A) Start off with your own **personal anecdote** on the prophetic and personal introductions (5 - 10 minutes), then ask who would like to be prophesied over first . .

B) Time guidelines –

We aim for 12 minutes on average per person, 60 minutes for all 5 - it's about **keeping it tight, but not rushing**!

- CHOOSE the person to be prophesied over
- WAIT **1-2 minutes** to receive word/revelation from the Holy Spirit
- EACH SHARE prophecy with the person and get their FEEDBACK up to **1-2 minutes** per person (about **8 minutes** total)
- PRAY for the person chosen **2 minutes** and begin again with choosing the next person

    (Sharing /feedback will probably take less than 2 minutes per person.)

NB. We'll also aim for you to have a buffer of an extra 10 minutes at the end to "keep in your wallet". If it is really, really, overflowing then you could also spill over into the break time.

C)
1. Our role as budding 'prophets' is more to administer, govern and guide the prophetic rather than necessarily prophesying ourselves; we release others into prophetic gifting and flow. Hold back where you can so you can steer others into releasing their prophetic words.
2. Protect the vulnerable; make sure this is SAFE encouraging words!
3. Do your best to ensure the heart of GOD is released
4. Gently steer away from control or overly directional words

5. Prophetic words given in this setting need not be "owned" by all those stepping into their gifting ie responsibility taken for them. CONTRAST this with words given by us as budding 'prophetic ministers' where we must be far more careful

Overall event coordinator notes:

- *i.   Need to emphasise seating with space between groups so not distracting*
- *ii. Pens, Phones & Papers*
- *iii. Slotting in late arrivals – introduce them to the group leaders*
- *iv. Gentle nudging time wise at 10 minutes ("2 minutes more") and then "ALL CHANGE"*

LESSON 7: "SOAKING" AND BEING "DRUNK IN THE SPIRIT"

If any thirst let Him come to me and drink.

Is any thirsty let him come.

Don't be filled with wine and drunk on wine BUT be filled and inebriated with The SPIRIT.

Come unto me and take my yoke upon you.

These are all invitations by GOD to come into His presence and REST, REFILL AND RECHARGE!

So what do we do when we are soaking?

   a. We rest, we lie down, we are in a position of rest

   b. We listen to worship, soft, anointed and inspiring worship (search for soaking worship online)

   c. We do not necessarily sing along to the music – we are called to rest and soak in, saturate in His presence and the divine atmosphere

   d. We keep our antennas up, to receive from The LORD, to travel in the spirit, to be totally open to Him

   e. We may choose to mediate on passages on travelling in the spirit and heavenly encounters like in the book of Ezekiel, Daniel and Revelation

   f. As we get filled with His SPIRIT we begin to feel light, to feel happy, to feel rekindled. This is drunkenness in the spirit

LESSON 8: ACTIVATIONS INTO THE SCREEN ON YOUR MIND, WORDS OF KNOWLEDGE, PROPHECY, TRAVELLING IN THE SPIRIT, DISCERNING OF SPIRITS AND MORE

SPIRITUAL GIFT ACTIVATIONS

A question we need to resolve in our hearts when it comes to pursuing the gifts of GOD is this – are we going to see the sovereign act on GOD's part an invitation into pursuing these manifestations as an act of faith on our part?

Paul told us repeatedly to "Desire the best gifts", our LORD JESUS when walking water by an act of His will was asked by Peter if he too could walk on water (perform the miraculous at will). The heart of GOD for His children was forever settled with His loving response to Peter -
"LORD if it is you, bid me come!" "COME!!"

So, what is an activation? Its simply a prayer we pray inviting The HOLY SPIRIT to impart to us the ability to move in a certain dimension of a spiritual gift.

The activation we would all be most familiar with is the activation into speaking in tongues. We lead the people in a biblical understanding of the gift, then in a prayer to be prayed in faith and then to expect a result. It is the same principles with all the activations.

1. **Locate the screen of your mind – your imagination**

Picture a dog / rose / garden / car (could be any of these)

Then ask for details (how to zoom in on your lens imagination)

This is where over 90% of revelation will come – onto the screen of your mind.

2. **Words of knowledge**

We have covered several in chapter – how to prophecy or more accurately for most of these activations how to receive a word of knowledge (since it is for most part present information not future information)

3. **Prophecy**

So, for this ask The HOLY SPIRIT what season someone is in; then ask for what season they are going into? (I learnt this one from Cheryl Fritz of INSIDE OUR PROPHETIC TRAINING)

4. **Prophesying to yourself**

Apart from through other people GOD also wants to speak to your directly! My sheep hear My voice, His word says. So get out a note pad. Clear your thoughts, submit your mind, will and emotions to Him and flow . . . a good first line is, "My child I love you and so cherish this moment to share to my heart with you . . ."

5. Travelling in the spirit

Ask someone in the group if you may come to their house. Then all of you pray and by grace and by choice go to their home and write down what you see. Eg type of furniture, colour of curtains etc….. ask the volunteer for feedback

SECTION B
GROWING INTO PROPHETIC MINISTRY
(9 hours)

Section introduction

This section is for those who now sense a calling to grow in prophetic grace beyond the average believer. Some of this is a call to be able to teach and empower others with what you are now walking in. The principles shared here if followed will empower you to walk in greater consistency and depth of revelation in your gifting. You will begin to understand who GOD not only wants to use your gift but also your life.

Personal notes

_____

_____

_____

LESSON 9: GROWING IN PROPHETIC FLOW

10 tools to more flow:-

1. Filled with The Word – several chapter of speed reading
2. Soaking
3. Stepping out and taking risks
4. Waiting on The LORD for WOKs before a meeting
5. Worshipping to build the atmosphere
6. Having a 'minstrel' playing as you prophesy
7. Praying in the spirit for hours
8. Fasting
9. Practise prophesying out – not to an individual, just releasing whatever GOD is giving you
10. Listen to the prophecies of more experienced prophetic ministers

Practical –

A) Glass of water and mints handy
B) No distractions
C) Listen to and hear what others are prophesying (to the same person)
D) Be comfortable
E) Take pauses for HOLY SPIRIT to release His Presence and the FATHER's love – aka encounter

CHARACTER, RISK & DEVELOPMENT ISSUES

1. "First steps to prophesying is a large dose of humility" Graham Cooke, "On average it takes 15 – 20 years to make a prophet"
   Prophesy out of humility and GOD will give grace to face any issue and put it right and correct it.

2. Be secure in your identity as opposed to your gift or ability to minister. Out of identity then PAPA GOD will release your destiny

3. Wilderness training periods for those called to prophetic ministry. Get used to handling rejection.

4. Differentiate between diagnosis and prognosis. WOK open up an issue, prophecy speaks into the heart of it, WOW how to respond to the issue. "Thank you FATHER I understand that about this person's life. Now in the light of that, what is it that you want to say to them?" (GC)

5. Avoid negativity and judgementalism. If we find it easy to give hard words, there's something wrong with our spirits

RISK & MESSES

"It is inevitable that people will make mistakes and go beyond their measure. When we are developing ministry and gifting we need to create an atmosphere where people are free to fail. If we insist on perfection or maturity in the early stages of development we will not cultivate people in the right manner" (Graham Cooke)

"Instead of faith to explore we will cause a fear that will hold back. Instead of boldness we will create intimidation. Instead of producing mature men and women we will cause their ministry to hit a ceiling and level off"

FAITH & PROPHECY

1Peter 4:10; Romans 12:6;

You never know all that The FATHER wishes to pass across in a message at the start of it. As you practice and grow accustomed to the etiquette around using your gifts you will grow more comfortable and confident in your gift.

_____

_____

_____

FAITH – *developing the faith muscle*

Luke 4:1, 14; Romans 8:14; Joshua 1:6; 2Corinthians 13:5; Romans 4:16-21; Jeremiah 15:16; Job 23:12

Allow the sprit to lead you into the wilderness places. When he says move, respond. If you get it wrong, don't worry – it is part of the process, learn and get back on track. Be bold, be courageous. How strong is your faith & trust now? Determine to move from weak faith to unwavering faith through to strong faith and ultimately to being fully persuaded! Grow your faith in the areas that it is weak in. Be deliberate. Double, treble, quadruple your Word intake.

Understanding negative prophetic revelation

Prophetic words are by nature directional – they speak about your future! Words of knowledge are about the present, where you are at now. When ministering in the prophetic, a negative word is not for them, it is always for you!, for you to steward, to guard to administer. It is given to you as a place of great privilege, for you to understand their struggle, the issue this person is going through. It is for you to let compassion flow through you towards them; so, don't ever prophesy this first thing you may see but the second. The second is the solution, the hope, the healing, the promise. Learn to wait and "pause for the cause"

LESSON 10: MORE GUIDELINES FOR UNDERSTANDING & GIVING PROPHECY

A. THE REVELATION, INTERPRETATION AND APPLICATION OF MATURE PROPHECY

Three Parts to understanding prophecy:

e.g. Acts 11:27-34

Agabus prophesied famine *(the revelation)*.

Others decided what God was trying to say *[interpretation]*

Then they decided what to do *(application)*

Acts 21:10-14 Agabus and prophecy concerning Paul *[wrong interpretation!]*

Two examples from Abraham and Sarah – work <u>with</u> God to bring about a prophecy. Isaac not Ishmael.

Romans 12:6 Take time with predictive prophecy to be sure it is from God. Let God work it out (not you) by co-operating with Him.

B. GUIDELINES FOR GIVING PROPHECY

    A. **Small group settings e.g. Home Groups**

This type of prophesying can often be more personal in nature as you can have a word for a specific person. The same guidelines as for large group meetings apply here but this is a better platform for growing in confidence.

    a) Firstly let's talk about what you could say as an introduction to what's on your heart in a natural way. Suggestions for intro's are
        i. "I sense The FATHER would like to say to you . .

ii. "I see this picture of a _____ every time I look at you .. would it be OK for me to pray for you?

b) In the intro you have now by your words or prayer brought The SPIRIT more on yourself and the atmosphere and can now go ahead more easily in the flow of what GOD is wanting to say, 'I love you my child, I am with you all the days of your life, I care for you and have a plan for you .."

c) So, again wait for and expect that flutter or nudge in your heart that let's you know that something is coming, you look at the person you are to prophecy over and from your heart cooperate in faith with The HOLY SPIRIT by saying what you sense is a particular word of encouragement for them

B. In large group settings e.g. worship service

a. Wait for that "flutter" in your heart, that sudden quickening of your pulse that is an indication that The SPIRIT is on you and desires to speak through you, then ..
b. Check to see if this is the right moment . . .
c. Wait a little while if it's not, (How do I know if it's a good time? Will you be interrupting someone else or something that The LORD is already doing .. is there a break or pause in the meeting?)
d. If no opportunity seems to be presenting itself, consider letting the leader of the meeting or his deputies know you've got a word from The LORD, you could do this by slipping a note to him or discreetly telling him.
e. Assuming you now have an opportunity to release what you've been given, you may need to pause a second as you again wait for the "surge" of The Spirit to come on you again.
f. Speak out the first words or describe the picture that you've been given and flow along as The SPIRIT gives or shows you more ..
g. STOP as soon as the river of words or pictures dries up.

C. When the word was received with the person not present

As is this less spontaneous there will be a greater fear of what if I'm wrong? If a personal word for someone, there are various opening lines that neutralize fear (or a tendency to pride if proven right) by protecting you from an expectation that you are 100% sure about the word you deliver. Only GOD is infallible. Opening lines for the delivery of such prophetic words may be to for instance say, 'I was praying for you the other day and felt very strongly in my heart that ..' Always good to have someone that that person trusts on hand to also weigh the word as you deliver it.

D. Other public settings

It is not always called for to speak out publicly in a meeting. Know when it is and when it is not. I've been able to deliver a word in pubic in a wedding before, but he couple getting married knew me well. Sometimes, it is best to simply write it on a piece of paper and offer it to the leadership; 'offer' being the functional word.

LESSON 11: MORE ON PROPHETIC FLOW & PROTOCOLS

Grasping the rules of engagement or niceties can eliminate most of the problems that prophetic people fall into. These are towards: -

   A. The LORD
   B. The person or people we prophesy to
   C. The leaders in the environment in which we are exercising our gift

1Thessalonians 5: 19-21; 1Corinthians 14:39-40

We must not despise prophecies. All things must first "be done" while we simultaneously think of the order (protocols) that go with it.

A. Towards The LORD

1Samuel 3:18; 2Kings 20:1-9

THE LORD ALWAYS DESIRES A RESPONSE – *a sense of responsibility for what HE's said. .*
Eli failed in this whereas Hezekiah understood how to respond

Very often in listening to The HOLY SPIRIT as HE helps us to interact with The FATHER it's similar to how a husband needs to read between the lines when his wife says something. We too need to also UNDERSTAND HIS voice and the meanings behind what we're hearing.

Luke 24:28,29; Mark 6:48

HE wants a response from you, don't just shrug your shoulders and walk away.

1Chronicles 11:17-19

We need to learn to respond to HIS slightest whispers.

B. Delivering personal words to people

Never assume that a word is 100% correct and to be received as absolute truth by the recipient. Leave room for shades of interpretation and your own flavourings of how you perceived and received the word. Know your area of operation and specialty in giving words. Know your track record.

Avoid delivering personal words without the company of other people to help the recipient weigh the word.

C. In an open congregational setting

Find out if open prophecy is welcome in the setting in which you are offering it before releasing it. Otherwise write it down and deliver it that way. Find out the personal preferences of the local church leadership where you are called to; how best would they like prophecies to be delivered?

D. Directional words to a congregation

This must be given to the leaders of the congregation unless the ministry is in under your jurisdiction i.e. you are in leadership over the assembly. Even so, they are best written down so that they do not murky up the waters and can be weighed properly by those with authority over the congregation.

THE PROPHETIC FLOW:

This is when anointed worship draws the presence of GOD upon a gathering leading the release of anointed words of prayer or prophecy. When this flow comes into a meeting it's often seen as a river flowing through the hall. A key purpose of the prophetic is to release people into prayer & action.

ENCOURAGING PROPHETIC WORDS

When the spirit of prophecy is "in the air" brooding over a meeting.

Sometimes you will know that The FATHER wishes to speak to us through a prophetic word but the spirit, unction or anointing of prophecy is in the air, but it's hanging, it's trying to come but not quite there yet. You can only really do something about this if you are leading the meeting. The two usual options are:-

   1. Silence, ask the people to be quite as you wait for the word to come. .
   2. Ask for a musician to strum on his guitar of play the keyboard.

Either of these will cause an increase of The Presence of GOD in the atmosphere releasing the prophetic word.

LESSON 12: CONDITIONAL & UNCONDITIONAL PROPHECY, PLUMBLINES

1Samuel 2:30; 1Kings 21:29; Isaiah 38:1-6

Not all prophecy is bound to happen, words can be conditional depending on the responses of people's hearts.

___

___

___

TRUE & FALSE PROPHETS

Numbers 23; Matthew 7:15-21; 1Corinthians 14:29

The LORD JESUS teaches us to judge prophets by the content of their character not the accuracy of their prophetic words.

It is expected that New Testament prophetic words are rarely 100% accurate. This is why we are told to weigh them. (See page 80)

How can we grow in accuracy?

    b. By practise

    c. By being accountable

    d. By allowing our hearts & motives to be continuously cleansed

    e. By knowing the nature of GOD more

    i. By being in close fellowship with other prophetic people

PROPHETIC DECEPTION – *idols in our hearts*

Scripture: Ezekiel 14:1-11; Numbers 22 – 25; 31:16; Romans 1:18 -32

When we allow an idol to remain in our hearts GOD Himself will allow us to remain in confusion and even compound the confusion we are in until by the grace of GOD we see that we are in trouble and repent.

Balaam didn't key into the need to not be deceived by our own hearts (Numbers 22:12, 20, 22-23) and almost died as a result of it. Purity of heart is so important if we are not to hear what we want to hear!! For some The LORD gives them up to their own desires, this can happen to believers too, beware! (Romans 1:28)

So, what's an idol? Anything that is in our heart that we love more than GOD. This could be one of our children, a spouse, the work of Christian ministry even! Very dangerous.

Yet another entrance for deception is when the word of GOD is clear about an issue but we choose to either ignore it or pray about it! Yes, it can be very dangerous to pray about things, which are already clearly stated in the word of GOD. The LORD may allow you to hear an answer in conformity with what you would like to hear even though it is wrong!

SCREENING PROPHETIC WORDS AND PICTURES

1Corinthians 13:9,10

Receiving: Sometimes a word can be so obscure and clouded by the style of the vessel that has brought it that it takes great grace to extract any substance from it! Keep trying, if confused ask for help from more mature ones. The 5% degree of truth embedded in it can well be worth the effort.

Giving: Do your best to understand your individual foibles and idiosyncrasies that often inadvertently make the picture of what The SPIRIT has given you cloudy and vague. Recognise these things in your delivery and even offer them as an appendix to the word. For example you may say, 'I hear GOD best in King James English, that's just how HE speaks to me / how my spirit man has been trained to hear HIS Voice.

LESSON 13: THE CALLING TO PROPHETIC MINISTRY

10 Things about Prophetic Ministry

1. It is perceiving
    a. Or seeing in the spirit with your imagination
    b. Feeling something strongly a powerful urge
    c. In a dream, in a vision
    d. A voice, a premonition

2. It is prayer
    a. Out of a response to what you have seen or perceived
    b. So a time of special prayer
    c. A desire to minister to someone in a healing line etc
    d. A time to be still and worship – "I perceive GOD is here in a unique way"

3. It is purpose
    a. Being unveiled
    b. This is what GOD is saying in this .
    c. This bible passage is saying this to us at this time
    d. I feel this is an opportunity to . .

4. It is releasing . .
    a. Courage
    b. Encouragement
    c. Faith
    d. A sense of divine awareness – GOD is not caught unawares
    e. Into all the 9 sp gifts

5. It is equipping
    a. Like all 5fold gifts and offices
    b. It is training

c. It is imparting

6. It is commissioning
   a. As in acts 13
   b. It is sending forth
   c. Notably when there is a prophetic presbytery
   d. A recognised level of authority and credence

7. It is managing
   a. The protocols of prophetic flow and release
   b. Character development
   c. Accountability

8. It is diverse
   a. Prophetic seers
   b. Prophetic speakers / naby
   c. Prophets to the church
   d. Prophets to the society
   e. Prophetic watchmen and interpreters of the signs of the age
   f. Prophetic counsellors
   g. Inner healing prophetic ministers
   h. Prophetic worship leaders
   i. Prophetic glory carriers
   j. Prophetic intercessors and prayer strategists
   k. Prophetic reformers

9. It is often a mix with other gifts notably the apostle
   a. Signs and wonders
   b. Revelation truths
   c. Building alongside others

10. It is an ascension gift of JESUS to His body

SECTION C SHADES OF PROPHETIC MINISTRY (8 hours)

Section introduction

Speaking about spiritual gifts, Paul says how there are diverse operations and administrations of the call of GOD. This is exemplified in the prophetic ministry. All ministries which rely mainly on the revelatory gifts falls into this setting. Examples of this are the worship ministry, prayer ministry, inner healing ministry, sings and wonders ministries, prophetic appointment ministries, watchman ministries are prime examples. Also in this category of prophetic ministries are prophetic reformers and social justice ministries.

Personal notes

LESSON 14: DISCERNING OF SPIRITS, DREAMS & VISIONS

The Discerning of spirits:

What it is: This is the supernatural ability to see or sense in the spirit realm. I include the term sense because our spirits are capable of being activated to touch, sight, smell, taste & hearing like our physical bodies.

What it's not: It is not an ability to be discerning or intuitively know someone's not right for the job for instance.

Examples

a. I drove up to a home and coming out of it was a minister who I was to meet for the first time, as I approached him I "saw" an ugly contorted face over his natural face, I knew that it was the face of lust on him. Later I found out from him that he had problems in this area.
b. I walked into someone's home in Phoenix, USA and saw on a particular spot that there was a 'fountain of grace' in her living room – later she confirmed this to be true.
c. In the company of my wife I went to visit a Christian lady and as I walked in could "smell" sin & immorality. Later again we realized that she had problems in this area.
d. Twice I have perceived The Cloud of GOD's Glory cloud in a Christian meeting, once I knew it was there, the other time my eyes opened to see it more clearly.
e. A sister in Herne Bay testifies to smelling the aroma of heaven in a meeting
f. Two people came into a meeting and felt that there feet were getting wet as they stood in the middle of the hall, when I mentioned that a river was flowing right through the hall they burst out laughing as it explained what they were physically feeling

_____

_____

PROPHETIC PICTURES, PROPHETIC DREAMS & VISIONS

Numbers 12:6-8
Four ways that The FATHER speak to us

Visions & Trances

Acts 10:3,10

DREAMS AND HOW TO INTERPRET THEM

Key facts

GOD speaks in dreams

Dream interpretation is a gift from GOD. As with all gifts is must be developed by our exercising it. Start by learning to interpret your own dreams.

The gift of interpretation often works with seasoned wisdom and understanding of the nature of GOD.

A dream is an invitation by GOD to participate in the outcome – its outcome is not inevitable. There are various categories of dreams.

Understanding symbols is key; pictures are worth a thousand words.
Discover typical symbols and their meanings.

Find the key thought pattern that GOD is seeking to communicate; don't be side tracked by the inconsequentials

Do ask the person questions like, "What emotion were you feeling when you saw such and such in the dream?"

1. The meaning of the dream is locked inside the spirit of the recipient. They know the meaning is correct when they are told it.

2. Wait on HOLY SPIRIT, lean on GOD for the meaning. Sometimes this will take a few moments to seep into your spirit

3. If nothing comes yet, let the person know you will get back to them. Don't offer what you are not convinced about.

***How do these all operate?** The HOLY SPIRIT comes upon you and empowers you for that moment or period of time to do things you can't do naturally.*

***How do we receive these gifts?** By desire, by pressing in - some things are both <u>TAUGHT</u> and <u>CAUGHT</u>!*

LESSON 15: PROPHETIC ACTIONS, WALKS & DRIVES & PROCLAMATIONS

PROPHETIC ACTIONS
Ezekiel
From time to time either as part of our praying or after prayer The SPIRIT may prompt us to do some physical action that is apparently related to our prayers. When we respond in faith and carry out these actions they release the power of GOD in mighty ways. The actions somehow act to release the power of GOD. Some of the more common actions are
1. Clapping – this is a like a release of power in warfare

2. Clicking fingers – again it is like determining that something prayed for is being done and things are being moved into place
3. Punching the air - there are times that The SPIRIT if GOD will instruct me to punch the air triumphantly as an act of victory.
4. Dance - What is it that makes dance in the spirit so powerful? It is done by a release of The SPIRIT of GOD, as we yield to it, it causes more of a release of The SPIRIT into the atmosphere. It is powerful, it breaks open the atmosphere, it ushers in The KING.
5. Waving flags – ushers in the presence of GOD in a greater measure

PROPHETIC WALKS & DRIVES
It is good to prayer walk, by this I mean, decide to pray over and around a territory. What makes it prophetic is the degree to which this walk was a) instigated of The SPIRIT and b) controlled by Him, or put another way the degree to which we were yielded to Him.
Once in Ibadan, Nigeria I was on my way to worship on a Sunday morning at the International Church that I pastured, I was due to to bring the message that morning. For some reason that day I went to our venue by public transport that particular day. This involved a change of taxi at a place called Mokola Roundabout. As I walked between the taxi terminals my spirit was 'arrested', I was drawn to make a detour and found myself going towards the bank of a river, the Ogunpa River that goes through most of the city. I knew that I needed to pray over the river, then to walk alongside it as I prayed. In time I realized that I would not make the service that morning. I eventually was called to walk along it for 4 hours all that way until it leaved the cities outskirts. As I prayed I made proclamations as I was led to. This ended with me issuing a call to rename the river from Ogunpa – 'the god of iron kills' to Idunnu 'Blessing'.

Similarly in Kent, UK I have often over a season been asked to drive along High Streets making proclamations.

PROPHETIC PROCLAMATIONS

Ezekiel 37

When Ezekiel was told to prophesy to the dead bones he was being asked to proclaim and declare a thing. This prophesying is creative in nature and is always based on what we have been shown by The HOLY SPIRIT. This is of course a different category of normal prophesying, where we give a word from GOD to someone to encourage them.
Whenever confronted with a situation, always look to spirit realm and be expectant for pictures and revelation. When we have seen this in the spirit realm we are empowered to release it with our mouths, in order to manifest it on the earth.

LESSON 16: PROPHETIC EVANGELISM, TREASURE HUNTS

Romans 10:14,15; Isaiah 52:7

An evangelist – one who heralds or brings good news. As with prophecy, being prophetic and the ministry of a prophet so being evangelistic does not mean we occupy the evangelists office. The HOLY SPIRIT gives us evangelistic hearts; it is left to The LORD as to whether we are called to function in the office or ministry of an evangelist. Usually if one is called to function in that office specifically there will be a wide spread recognition accompanied with above average results. This does not take away from the fact that we are all called to be evangelistic, i.e to have a heart inclination to spread The Word of GOD.

WHY EVANGELISE?
So, why do we evangelise? Do we need to evangelise?
For several reasons: -
We are instructed to (Matthew 28:18-20; Mark 16:15-16)
We have been equipped to (Matthew 28:18, Luke 4:18, 36; 9:1-2)
The Love of GOD in our hearts compels us to (2Corinthians 5:14)
We do not want to carry guilt for not letting others around us know what we know (Ezekiel 33)
Our churches often will not grow without effectively reaching out to new people to come in (Acts 2)
Soul winning comes from being wise and also requires wisdom (Proverbs 11:30)

EVANGELISM
When we think of evangelism all sorts of things can come to mind – handing out tracts (Christian literature) on street corners, using a megaphone to warn people about hell, having heated debates about the authenticity of scripture, knocking on doors to see if someone wants a prayer etc most of which fills us with dread! Evangelism can be very unpleasant to say the least when done as a form of cold calling.

WHY BOTHER?

Matthew 13; Mark 4; Luke 8; 1Corinthians 3:6

Let's be clear as to our own part and The LORD's part. We sow the seeds, we water the seeds but it is HIS part to grant increase. The parable of the sower seems to suggest that 25% success rate seems to be quite good!

1Corinthians 15:6; Acts 1:15

Despite over 500 seeing the resurrected LORD only 120 gathered on the day of Pentecost.

Romans 9:16; John 6:37;

Our duty is to offer the gospel, to sow the seeds. Let's keep a healthy balance as to our role and HIS.

PRESSURE OFF!
Acts 10; 8:26-40; Matthew 11:28-30

Understandably we often feel compelled to reach out and some times feel very guilty if we don't end up talking to others about The LORD. Yes, we ought to have a sense of responsibility to reach out but then we ultimately need to lean on HIS Grace to help us to do so effectively.

So RELAX! Sit back and relax. Pressure off. Why? Because when we do things HIS way our burden becomes easy and HIS yoke light. There's another way to do evangelism that is natural and easy and dare I say FUN! Yes, FUN!

Let's look at a few examples of this in Acts Peter had a trance, and then The SPIRIT told him that he was going on an errand. Scarcely had he taken this in when there was a knock on the door and some people had sent for him, again he was asked to go along with them. What followed was as he preached JESUS The HOLY SPIRIT without reference to him, fell on all who were listening! Wow! How wonderful is that! Listen to what The SPIRIT is saying and obey HIM and see results! Wow!

The other example is of Phillip, told to go to a dessert road, then to run after a chariot then caught away miraculously to somewhere else to continue preaching! Splendid!

Can this happen to us today? Well, we are told that these things are written for our instruction, our training, our admonition, and our warning! So I say YES! If it happened then, then it is to point us in the same direction and inspire faith and courage to go do the same!

Evangelism without The SPIRIT is hard- it is like cold calling! Now, The SPIRIT gives life, the movement of The SPIRIT is likened to a flow, to the movement of a river, the touch of a breeze. Evangelism without The SPIRIT is hard, it can be like a rote exercise, and it can be as we all know off putting to those we are trying to reach as well as to us trying to reach them!

The aim of this lesson on PROPHETIC EVANGELISM is to take the graft out of EVANGELISM. Now, we will still need faith & courage to evangelise, we will still need diligence to use the opportunities that will come across our path, we will still need to live lives that are an advert

for HIS Kingdom and yes, we will be required to be sensitive to The SPIRIT, but after all aren't these qualities we should be pressing into anyway?

Come along for the ride!

So, what is PROPHETIC EVANGELISM?

John 1:47-49; 4:1-26

The SPIRIT of GOD gives The LORD JESUS words of knowledge for these two people helping them to grow in and discover faith in HIM.

So what's Prophetic Evangelism? Let's look at these two words separately.

Ephesians 5:18-21; 1Corinthians 12:3;

It is EVANGELISM with a very crucial bit – "prophetic" added on! Let's look at the other word – 'PROPHETIC'

Prophetic refers to, *"In the flow of The HOLY SPIRIT, under the influence of The SPIRIT"* - this could be in a word, a message preached, a prayer or an action or a piece of art etc. The dictionary defines it as "of, belonging to, or characteristic of prophecy or foretelling events as if by divine inspiration" Now it helps us to remember that in the New Testament prophecy is more *forthtelling* than *foretelling*. It is speaking under the inspiration of The SPIRIT to bring encouragement and inspiration. Some of this will be futuristic, some will be an uplifting word for now.

Looking at our earlier definition, "under the influence of", Paul admonishes the church to not be filled to excess with wine which leads to debauchery but rather to be filled with The SPIRIT! The outcome? Speaking joyfully to one another, music playing in our hearts, overflow of joy and the other fruits which communion and being intoxicated with The SPIRIT release – PEACE, LOVE, KINDNESS etc.

In a nutshell, **PROPHETIC EVANGELISM is evangelising under the influence**! It is reaching out to our world with the joy and gaiety that comes from being touched and influenced by The SPIRIT of GOD. This is so very different from trying to coerce people into something, from the angst that straining and striving often produces.

Getting under and staying under the influence, where our words are full of boldness like Peter and the early apostles, where it is evident that we have "been with JESUS" is what we attempt to transmit in the rest of this course –

Learning to pray, to be sensitive to The SPIRIT, to walk in the authority that we've been given to pray for the sick and to represent HIS Kingdom on Earth. This is all part of the vital mixture that will make us active and fruitful bearers of glad tidings to our friends, neighbours and communities.

LESSON 17: PROPHETIC EVANGELISM (2) Practicals, Tips & Pointers

"DREAM INTERPRETATION", "A PERSONAL PROPHETIC WORD" etc
These forms of evangelism rely on the prophetic grace that we have been blessed with. Place a poster in a busy area of the town offering these "services". Lean on The HOLY SPIRIT to give interpretation to the dreams – a good thing about it is, it's their dream we're interpreting!

THE TREASURE HUNT
The Treasure Hunt came out of Bethel Church in Redding, California. A very good resource is "The Ultimate Treasure Hunt" by Kevin Dedmon.

Basically we: -

1. Split into groups of 3 – 4 persons each. (*this is a good number to be able to bounce things off one another*)

Note: Good to have a gender and age mix; kids can be good at thinking out of the box to chase down the clues we've been given.

2. Ask The LORD for words of knowledge, which are the clues for the Hunt.

Note: It's best to give a time limit of 5 minutes for this so we don't begin to wonder if a word was from GOD or not. We learn by practise where our imagination stops and prophetic words, pictures & words of knowledge kick in. *(Hebrews 6:14)*

3. Look for clues in five categories: -

    a. A geographical location – where are they?

    b. Articles of clothing, shirt colour etc. what do they look like?

    c. Their name? Male or female?

    d. What area they may need grace & prayer in - healing? a marriage or relationship issue?

    e. Anything unusual or out of the ordinary?

Note: things we are not sure on write to the side of your main list.

4. Share with each other the clues we've been given. These clues should be written on the back of your Hunt paper so that you're aware of the clues your team members have got.

Note: Remember to be aware of what each other has written down

5. Go out starting at the locations we've got look for our clues.

Note: Don't get stuck on the (location) clue, it may be that our treasure is to be found en-route to the clue.

6. Be sensitive to one another, to what each other are feeling. Be careful also to not talk over one another's heads when talking to your treasure.

7. Approach the treasure. With great joy, gentleness and non-threatening politeness! Seek to build relationship with them, how would you approach someone you wanted to make friends with? Good intro statements may be: -

    a. Hi, my names _____ and we're Christians from the town who are out on a treasure hunt and we believe you may be the treasure we've been looking for.

Hiya, is your name _____?
Hi this may seem a little odd but _____

A. TIPS

    a. Practise is needed in order to grow in faith & confidence *EXPECTING* to see our clues
    b. Then we grow in *BOLDNESS* to jump at these occasions as we are sometimes so delighted to actually have seen the clues that we then start explaining to the group what we've seen - as the clues pass us by!
    c. We also learn to *NOT BE FIXATED* on the clues themselves but to *KEEP ALERT* for anyone that The LORD may highlight to us as we go in search of them.
    d. The clues *MOBILISE* us and get us out there with our sprits being *TRAINED* to be sensitive to The SPIRIT's leadings.
    e. Over all it is a thrilling experience to be out there on the hunt as we grow in out dependence on the leading and guidance of The HOLY SPIRIT.

B. Also . . . .

- Keep your ears open to receive fresh insight from The SPIRIT when interacting with our treasure
- Good to keep an hour for worship & intercession

C. Timing issues

- For regular meetings it looks something like this . .
    - Worship & Intercession — 1 hour
    - Prophetic activation — 15 minutes
    - Equipping — 15 minutes
    - Clues — 15 minutes
    - Hunt — 1 hour
    - Testimonies — 15 minutes
    - TOTAL *- 3 hours*

BOLDNESS & INTIMACY
Go out full of: -

1. The JOY of The LORD
2. Expectancy for a divine encounter with someone
3. The FATHER's LOVE, care and compassion

Be equipped with

4. A word from The LORD for someone
5. A heart full of The SPIRIT
6. A testimony of The FATHER's goodness

Determine to: -

7. Keep things simple, avoid confusing "Christianese" language, culture and custom
8. Be sensitive as to who The LORD is *"highlighting"* – pointing out to you as needing your attention.
9. Step out in faith as you see clues you've received earlier

E. FEAR & BOLDNESS?

Antidotes to Fear & Intimidation

Romans; 1John 4:18; Proverbs 28:1; Hebrews 10:25; Ephesians 6
1. Walking in "The SPIRIT"
2. Walking in the love of GOD.
3. Walking in righteousness.
4. Walking in fellowship with other believers.
5. Walking with "full spiritual body armour" on.

LESSON 18: PROPHETIC DEPARTMENTS

Prayer

Intercession

Worship

Social justice

Deliverance ministry

Counselling ministry

Prophetic appointments

Prophetic training and equipping

Signs and wonders

Fasting

Prophets to nations

Prophets to the church

Prophetic actions

Warfare

24-7 worship

SECTION D
THE OFFICE OF A PROPHET
(5 hours)

Section introduction

This is a ministry calling from The LORD JESUS CHRIST. It is a very privileged place to occupy, speaking on behalf of GOD and speaking into the lives of men, churches, organisations and nations. it is a position which is open to abuse and manipulation by those who do not position themselves relationally so as to be held accountable. The preparation period and experiences that all who are called to this office is generally very long and demanding.

Personal notes

_____

_____

_____

LESSON 19: THE PREPARATION OF A PROPHET

a. The Preparation of The Prophet

The Prophetic Office carries a lot of responsibility and authority. As such it needs a lot of preparation, here we look at how God prepares His prophets before they are permitted to take up their office in the Body of Christ. Before they can be placed into office, they are trained, and then tested to see if they are able to handle the responsibilities.

1. *Must be trained and tested*

You cannot place dangerous tools in the hands of a child or one who is unskilled and irresponsible in their use. So also, God cannot place the tools and authority of the Prophetic Office into the hands of one who has not been correctly trained and become responsible enough to use them wisely.

This actually applies to all of the 5-fold ministry offices, but since the Prophetic Office carries a far greater power of authority than the others, except for the Apostolic Office, the preparation of the Prophet is unlike any of the others.

Most apostles tend to go also through the prophetic preparation on the way to qualifying for the apostolic office, so what I am going to share here applies very much also to the preparation of the Apostle.

2. *Must Hear Correctly*

It is very important that the prophet hears correctly before he opens his mouth. And that takes a bit of training and development. He must distinguish his own burden and prejudices from the pure word of God.

3. *Goes through God's Own Training*

So, God puts the prophet through a training that causes him to come to a place where he cannot rely on his natural abilities. Even his ability to hear the voice of God must be put in question, that he may never boast in himself. He must learn not to rely on the flesh in any of its forms, for then he will be subject to being influenced by the enemy.

He cannot rely on his mental, emotional or willpower capabilities. He cannot rely on his physical prowess or intelligence. He must become simply a channel through which the Spirit of God can speak.

4. His Preparation is not for Perfection

Since we all at times walk in the flesh and miss God, the prophet will never come to a place of sinless perfection. And that is not at all the goal of the prophetic preparation. The way God prepares His prophets is not to make them perfect, but to show them in no uncertain terms how weak and imperfect they really are. Until they come to the place where they walk humbly before Him in total dependence on Him alone. Where they speak with confidence, yet in fear and trembling.

b. What is Prophecy?

It is Communication for the Lord which can take many different forms: The Lord reveals

His Heart

His Thoughts

His Feelings

His Invitations

His Decisions

And future plans for the People of the Earth

c. Who Is the Prophet?

The prophet is one who hears from God and speaks forth His Word into the earth. When he (or she, I am speaking as a man so I am using the male gender here) speaks it forth. It is sent as a creative word as described by Isaiah the prophet Isaiah 55:11 *So shall my word be that goes forth out of my mouth: it shall not return to me empty, but it shall accomplish that which I please, and it shall succeed [in the thing] for which I sent it.*

When the prophet of God makes a declaration, he does not simply predict or indicate the will of God, but he literally speaks forth a decree into the earth.

And that word is sent forth in power to make things happen. We will discuss this more when we consider the ministry of Intercession, which is the hallmark of the prophetic ministry.

d. How Does God Prepare His Prophets?

Let's look then at how God prepares his prophets and apostles. One of the best passages that describes this is found in Paul's second letter to the Corinthians. 2 Corinthians 4:5-18.

5. For we preach not ourselves, but Christ Jesus the Lord; and ourselves your servants for Jesus' sake. 6 For God, who commanded the light to shine out of darkness, has shined in our hearts, to [give] the light of the knowledge of the glory of God in the face of Jesus Christ. 7 But we have this treasure in earthen vessels, that the excellence of the power may be from God, and not from us. 8 [We are] troubled on every side, yet not distressed; [we are] perplexed, but not in despair; 9 Persecuted, but not forsaken; cast down, but not destroyed; 10 Always bearing about in the body the dying of the Lord Jesus, that the life also of Jesus might be

made manifest in our body. 11 For we which live are always delivered over to death for Jesus' sake, that the life also of Jesus might be made manifest in our mortal flesh. 12 So then death works in us, but life in you. 13 We having the same spirit of faith, according as it is written, I believed, and therefore have I spoken; we also believe, and therefore speak; 14 Knowing that he which raised up the Lord Jesus shall raise up us also by Jesus, and shall present [us] with you. 15 For all things [are] for your sakes, that the abundant grace might through the thanksgiving of many rebound to the glory of God. 16 For which cause we do not faint; but though our outward man is perishing, yet the inward [man] is renewed day by day. 17 For our light affliction, which is but for a moment, produces for us a far more exceeding [and] eternal weight of glory; 18 While we look not at the things which are seen, but at the things which are not seen: for the things which are seen [are] temporal; but the things which are not seen [are] eternal.

I am going to look at some of the verses from this passage and discuss each aspect as it relates to the preparation of the prophet.

e. Caution! – Watch the Flesh!

For many who are called to the Prophetic Office there is an excitement at the prospect of becoming one who speaks for God and stands forth as one elevated to such an office. You expect God to grant great and wonderful revelations, and as you speak them forth people will stand in awe and wonder and wish they had the privilege you have been given. Imagine being able to tell people what God's purpose is for their lives? Imagine being able to pray for someone and have God reveal to you things about that person that they did not tell you. Imagine being able to release the blessing of God into the lives of others. It certainly seems like a very exciting calling.

But for most who receive this call, there comes a sudden shock when they find themselves being rejected, despised and ostracized because of their ministry. Instead of people admiring you and respecting the authority that God has placed in you, you suddenly find yourself being opposed and put down.

No one seems to understand the burden that burns in you. And when you speak forth the Prophetic Word, those who know you are quick to put it down and tell you that you are out of order, or that you have missed it. And then to top it off, it turns out that they are sometimes correct. You open your mouth to speak what you thought was a Word from the Lord, and you are way out in left
field.

1. Everything Starts to go wrong

……[We are] troubled on every side, yet not distressed;

What is happening here?

You are starting to enter into the preparation phase for the office of prophet. And the first sign of this is when everything in your life starts to go wrong. That's right, your life looks as though it is coming apart.

In Paul's words in this passage, you are troubled on every side. You know what it is like when you get up in the morning and it is one of those days when you wish you had stayed in bed. Everything you touch turns sour. Your family members all seem to be against you. Your spouse starts to fight with you. And when you arrive at work the boss and your fellow workers seem to pick up on it. You go to church hoping for some relief and the Pastor and other church members seem to have caught the vision too and feel they have been called to put you in your place.

Ever been there? If you are called to be a prophet then I know you have been there. Infact if you have not been there, then something is wrong somewhere. Perhaps you weren't called to be a prophet after all.

And I want to tell you what happens when everything in your life goes wrong like this. The first part of you that starts to let you down is your emotions. You feel so low that you begin to despair of life. You loose all desires and motivation to do anything significant. You begin to wonder even if the call to be a prophet was not just something you made up or imagined. So, the first and most significant part of your soul life is put out of action. But the Scripture tells you that you do not need to be distressed. When all this starts to happen, you don't have to throw your hands up in despair and give up. You realize that the Lord is in a most wonderful way, is starting to make you into a vessel that is fit for His use. He is starting to put the earthen vessel into the fire to make it into something beautiful. Have you never seen what a clay pot looks like before they bake it? It lacks all the shine and beautiful colours that it should have. They have been painted on, but they do not begin to show up until the pot has been put into the fire. Then the glaze and the colours start to show.

2. Dealing with your own mind

…..[we are] perplexed, but not in despair

Once your emotions have been put out of action, the next thing that God has to deal with is your ability to figure your way out of things. One of the things that often stands in the way of the prophet clearly hearing the voice of God is the voice of his own mind.
Your mind has a habit of subjecting everything you receive from the spirit to its own close scrutiny and analysis. You try to reason out what God is saying and why He is saying it and try to make sense of the Word He has given you. But this tendency, especially in those who are prone to the analytical temperamental traits, can become a great hindrance to the pure flow of prophetic revelation. So, what happens? You are brought into circumstances that defy all logic and explanation. The Lord leads you into situations that predispose you to things that bring total confusion in your mind, until you end up so perplexed by your situation that you cannot figure your way out. There just is no solution to the problem. This can take many forms. It can be a financial crisis or an interpersonal relationship crisis, etc.
But whatever it is, you can be sure that it will cause you to be backed into a corner, and there will be no natural way out. In this season you need a spiritual father that will just be there for you. Not to sympathize with you. But is spiritual enough to know what is going on not to interfere with divine protocols but just be both praying for you and gently guiding.
You will have to give up trying to find your own solution.

But once again, you do not have to end up in despair. You do not have to throw up your hands and wish you had never been born, like Job did when everything went wrong in his life. All that is happening is that the Lord is trying to get your attention. He is trying to tell you that you cannot rely on your natural mental capabilities. That these will let you down, but His Word will never let you down. A time to dig deep into His Word. He wants you to realize that your ability to be a prophet has nothing to do with your keen mind.

3. Opposition from Within

…..Persecuted, but not forsaken

As if all of that is not bad enough, the next thing you find appearing in your life is opposition from people who you thought would support you. Of course, you expected opposition from the world. You probably even expected it from those who are not walking closely with the Lord. You certainly expected it from those whom you rebuked because of their sin. But that is not where it comes from. It comes from within the fold. It comes from those who are the closest to you, and from whom you expected the greatest support and understanding. It will come from your own family members and those who are close to you. It will come from your own spiritual leadership and close friends and family of God.

And do you know what happens when people start to persecute you? They force you to do what they think is right, and they prevent you from doing what you want to do. Your ability to choose your own way is blocked. In other words, your free will is put out of action. Now you cannot freely make any choices for yourself. Instead you are forced to follow the choices of others.

Can you see what has happened now?

The first two things we spoke of put your *emotions* and your *mind* out of action. Now this one puts your *will* out of action.
That means that *emotions*, *mind* and *will* are all put on hold.

These are the three functions of the soul, and when they are all blocked, your soul life is put out of action and brought to a condition of death. At this stage you can say you are ready to be placed on altar.

But once more there is hope even in this situation. Because although it looks like the whole world is against you and no one is standing with you, the Word says that you are not forsaken. There is still one who is there for you. And if you will just reach out your hand to Him, He will take it and lead you on. But now you will be led like a blind person. You will not be able to rely on your own senses, but only on His leading.

Remember the senses take the reality away from the Word, always let the Spirit gain ascendency over the senses so that the Word will have its place in your circumstance. You won't be able to go by what you feel. You won't be able to go by what you think. You won't be able to go by what you choose. But you will only be able to follow as He leads. And that is the place He wants to bring you to.

4. Freedom from need of public recognition.

….cast down, but not destroyed

Well, you might think that all we have looked at so far is about as much as any person can take, but I have some bad news for you. It is not over yet. Because you see, the self-life that is in you is still alive and well. And although you might be forced to walk humbly before the Lord, there still remains that deep inner need for recognition. This is a big pit-fall most that operate in the prophetic. It is the one thing that drives us all to achieve in this life. We push ourselves beyond our limits at times, so that we can somehow succeed and receive the rewards of our success – *recognition from man*. As a preacher and servant of God, you cry out for the time when you can successfully proclaim the Word of the Lord and have others tell you how well you did. Is this pride? Not necessarily. It is just the way we are. And if you speak to any successful person you will find that this is the strongest motivation they have. It is seldom money that makes a person strive to succeed, whether in work, education or physical accomplishments. It is the deep cry for recognition from others. And the acclaim that comes with being praised for your efforts makes it worth all the time and labour you spent getting there. Without this motivation few would ever succeed in anything in life. But for the prophet, this motivation must bow to the call of God and the faithful proclamation of the Word. Often the faithful discharge of the prophet's duties will lead to the complete opposite. The prophets of the Old Covenant knew this only too well. Many of them were stoned to death and humiliated and treated shamefully because of their faithfulness to their ministry. And that is exactly what will happen when you are put through the prophetic preparation. You will be cast down, or humiliated. This can take place either by others putting you down, or it can take place by you opening your mouth and declaring something totally false or out of order.

You could find yourself wanting to sneak out the back way without anyone noticing. You feel like you could crawl under the door while it is still closed. It is not a pleasant experience.

But whichever form it takes, be sure that it will happen to you. You can count on it. Why? So that your ministry can never depend on or be influenced by your need for recognition.

If it were, then you cannot speak the unadulterated word of God. You will temper the prophetic word with your own ideas and fail to speak forth the truth for fear that people will reject you for it. And once again the promise is there that though you might go through this painful experience, you will not be destroyed. The Lord does not want to take away this thing from you. As a matter of fact, He delights in giving you all the recognition you deserve. But like all other things, it must first be brought to the cross.

5. The Loss of All Things Dear

v10, Always bearing about in the body the dying of the Lord Jesus, that the life also of Jesus might be made manifest in our body.

Well, are we there yet? Is it over yet? Am I ready to be a prophet now? Well almost, but not quite. You see, although the soulish life is the greatest hindrance to hearing clearly from the Spirit of God that dwells in your spirit, it is not simply the soul that is the problem. It is the tendency of the soul to submit to the body instead of the spirit. This is what the Bible calls 'walking in the flesh.

The body has desires of its own, which when allowed to dominate our lives result in the root causes of all spiritual problems. You can see this in studies in Counselling.

When the natural bodily desires of nourishment, reproduction and self-preservation come to dominate our lives, they give rise to covetousness, lust and bitterness. So, the body must also be brought into subjection. That does not mean that God is going to permit sickness and disease to come upon you. We are redeemed from these things, which are part of the curse of the law. However, it is likely that you will be led into a situation that could cause your body to come under attack. And you will find yourself facing situations where you cannot eat the food that you desire. Where you cannot fulfil the passions even in marriage, and where you are unable to defend yourself. You end up like the Scriptures describe Jesus, a sheep dumb before its shearers, a lamb being led to the slaughter.

The chances are that you will face the loss of all things that are dear to you. Those sentimental possessions that you have gathered over the years that mean so much to you, are things that prevent you from being free to do the will of God. The house that you built and spent years renovating might be stopping you from traveling to where God wants you to go. You might even face a choice of rescuing your marriage or going with the call of God. Because your partner might decide to reject that call and force you to do the same. You might have to leave the community where you grew up.

You might have to give up the career that you worked so hard for. All the things that make for a comfortable physical existence are likely to be put in question, and you might have to make some difficult choices to continue in the path of God's calling in your life. Because you see, the Lord is bringing you to death of all things and every part of you that stands in the way of you carrying out His call effectively will have to bow before the desire to put God's Kingdom first in your life. When Jesus was crucified on the cross of Calvary He faced terrific physical pain, but He also faced much more than that. He faced rejection by His own people. He faced the torture and humiliation of the Roman soldiers. He was deserted by those who loved Him. And then He was publicly humiliated as they stripped Him nearly naked and took away even the very clothes that

He wore.But the height of His suffering was as He hung there on the cross and turned towards the only One who really cared for Him and on whom He could rely – His heavenly Father. And that was when He faced the most painful part of His death. Because even the Father turned His back and looked the other way.

But our Saviour showed us how to die. He cried out with a loud voice. "It is finished." And then He handed himself over to the Father and gave up His spirit. People didn't usually die this way on the cross. They would hang and suffer there until they became exhausted from struggling to stay alive. They would continually push themselves up on the cross by their feet so that they could still breathe. Only when exhaustion set in and they had no more energy left would they stop doing this, and then they would suffocate to death. That is why the Romans decided to break the legs of the prisoners when Jesus was crucified, so that they would die more quickly.

Now what is the Lord teaching us from His death by crucifixion? Paul said in Galatians 2:20 *"I have been crucified with Christ."*

He was speaking about us becoming identified with Jesus in His death. And although our old nature was nailed to the cross with Jesus, and we by faith now reach out and take that death and apply it to ourselves, it takes an experimental application of the cross to our lives to cause sin to be dealt with in the flesh.

By Position, we are dead to sin, and alive to God. And legally we are considered as righteous before God because of what Jesus did on the cross. And since Jesus paid the price for our sins, we do not come into judgment for our sin, though we still fail and sin daily.

We are delivered once and for all from the guilt and penalty of our sin, because of the Finished Work of Calvary. But we find that sin still has a power in our life. Paul describes in Romans 7 the experience of one who is trying to live righteously but find himself still doing the very sin that he hates. So, sin is still there in our bodies. Its power still seems to follow us. And the Christian life is one of coming to grips with the power of sin and overcoming it. It involves a practical application of the cross to our experience, so that sin no longer has any power or influence in us. Until one day when Jesus returns, we will be transformed and receive our glorified and sinless bodies. And finally, we will be totally free from sin and live eternally in His presence in a state of sinless perfection.

These three things are what are known as the three tenses of salvation, and they are dealt with in detail under the heading of Soteriology – the doctrines of salvation. It is the *past*, *present* and *future* of salvation, and can be stated like this.

- **Past Tense** - I have been saved eternally from the guilt and consequences of sin because of Calvary.

- **Present Tense** – I am daily being saved from the power of sin in my life.

- **Future Tense** – I will one day be totally saved from the presence of sin.

We live in the present tense of salvation, and this is a continual process. And for the prophet of God, this becomes abundantly more obvious than it does in the life of the ordinary believer.

You see there has to come death to all of those things that prevent the prophet from operating efficiently. And then there can come a resurrection as God's power is released to shine forth.But the prophet must make a choice in the matter. God does not willingly subject us to the pressures needed to bring about that death. You see no one can experience the death of the cross alone. You cannot commit suicide by crucifixion. You can only hold up your hands and invite someone to nail you to the cross. And if you wish to go through the preparation and the death that it entails, then you have to commit yourself to the Lord and invite Him to prepare you.

And when you do this, you can expect to feel some nails being driven in. You can expect to have someone spit in your face, and push a crown of thorns on your head. And you can expect those who are closest to you to desert you. But the final death can only come when you make a choice to let go. While you push up on the cross and struggle to stay alive, the pain will only continue. But when you can with the Lord Jesus declare, "It is finished," and yield up your spirit in death, then it will end. And there will come a season in the grave followed by the victorious resurrection of your ministry in the fullness of power. If you don't allow this to happen, then you become a candidate for leg breaking. And the Lord has to take drastic measures to bring you fully to the end of yourself.

My Brothers and sisters you are reading this study as one who has been called by God to the Prophetic Office. And if this was a true calling, you know and acknowledge that what I have said is true. And you have been going through the mill. The pressure has been on, probably for a long period of time already.

The chances are you are totally confused by all of this and do not understand what has been happening. That is why I have prepared this study to make it clearer for you. And I want to assure you now that it is not necessary for the pain to continue. You can end it all very quickly by recognizing what God is telling you and coming to the end.

f. Stop Struggling

You must stop struggling and yield to what has been happening. When you are falsely accused you must not try to defend yourself and seek justification or vindication. But you must submit yourself humbly and die. And when you do this, all the turmoil will cease. The noise will disappear. And there will come a calm such as you have never known in a long time. And there will come a deep stirring inside you that you will not be able to understand.

Now is the time to let go of all effort and ministry. Infact you would probably do better to avoid any kind of spiritual activity at all. Just get involved in something secular. And leave the Lord to do His work in secret, because the body is now
placed in the tomb.

Jesus spent three full days in the tomb, and during that period He accomplished our redemption from the powers of darkness. They thought they had defeated Him, but on the third day He arose triumphant, with power and authority, having the keys of death and Hades. He was given the Name above every other name. And He took His place in heaven, sending forth the power of the Holy Spirit upon the church and interceding at the right hand of the Father. So, once you have gone through death, there will come a waiting period, where you will remain in the grave. And nothing will seem to be happening.

g. A new dawn

Do not let it concern you, because things are happening that you cannot see. Just wait for the resurrection, for it will surely come. And when it comes, there will come a new power and a new authority. And suddenly your ministry will spring forth in power and authority. And you will rise up to take your place as a fully-fledged Prophet of God.

Of course, that is not the end. There will be further times of training and further deaths to go through. Each new stage in your development will follow a very similar trend. But each one will also bring a greater depth of understanding and involvement in the Body of Christ. You might ask me, "How do you know this is true? How can you be sure that this is the way God works in preparing His prophets?" Well I have shown you from the Scriptures, but you can rest assured that this servant of God has been there many times. And I have worked with other God's prophets. And I have seen the process repeated in each one that has gone on for God and moved into a place of authority in the Kingdom of God. If you desire to move into that office my brother, then there is no easy way around. Just as Jesus had to go the way of the cross, so you and I will have to walk that way with Him if we aspire to the office of one who would speak forth the Words of Almighty God into the earth.

(By Wilfred Achumba)

LESSON 20: THE MINISTRY OF A PROPHET

IPAA DEFINITION AND CRITERIA OF A PROPHET

Definition of a prophet

One called and commissioned by The LORD JESUS and gifted by The HOLY SPIRIT with supernatural grace to be able to consistently interact with and impact the spiritual realm through revelations, prayers, prophetic acts, utterances, worship, construction of altars and so forth

Attributes of a prophet will often include grace to operate in all three revelatory gifts – word of knowledge, word of wisdom and discerning of spirits
as well as the utterance gifts
– tongues, interpretation of tongues and prophecy.
They will often have a passion and great affinity for abiding in GOD's Presence and receive supernatural visitations.
(*Luke 2:36-37*)

10 Classifications of PROPHETS

1. Prayer Leaders
2. Worship Leaders (1Chron 25:1-3)
3. Gift Equippers (Eph 4;1-13)
4. Commissioning (Acts 13:1-3)
5. Predictive (Acts 11, 19)
6. Writing (OT authors)
7. National Prophets (Jeremiah 1)
8. Church Prophets
9. Prophets to Society
10. Dream Interpreters (Gen 40:8)

Various functions of prophetic ministry –

- To train, equip and release others in the gift of prophecy
- To monitor the spiritual atmosphere and give a call to prayer accordingly
- To enhance the flow of release of the gifts of The SPIRIT in a meeting and provide and maintain the right atmosphere for this
- To declare the word of The LORD to their assigned sphere of influence
- To set up prayer and worship altars
- To lead in prophetic prayer actions

1. From gift of HOLY SPIRIT to gift from The LORD JESUS
   Gift of Prophecy – gift from HS, something we do, edifies and encourages; office of prophet – gift from JESUS, something you are, to direct, govern, correct, equip saints in

2. From occasional use to regular use
   We move from occasional words of prophecy (steeping into the waters) to frequent prophetic words and managing the gift of prophecy in others (being responsible for keeping the waters flowing) to as the case may be called the office of a prophet where you guard and deepen and widen the flow.

3. From exhortational "full stop" to exhortational plus directional words. Growth in revelation (Discerning of spirits, WOK's & WOW's) indicates moving into prophetic ministry from occasional use of prophecy

4. From out of our spirits to out of our spirit, soul and body
   "when the motivation of our ministry moves from compassion and love to helping us feel valuable and worthwhile, the entire ministry becomes polluted and the impact dramatically weakened" (Kris Vallaton) The character of the prophet plays a central role. "We must insist on a framework for the development of character" Graham Cooke

5. The roles of prophets : -
    a. To equip others to prophesy and hear GOD
    b. To handle the protocols, frameworks and use of prophetic gifting
    c. To bring
        i. Fresh direction to a church, movement or nation

        ii. Correction to a church, movement or nation

    d. To act as a catalyst

6. We prophesy spirit, soul and body!
   Hebrews 4:12 refers to the dividing of all three. Not from one another but from earthly, carnal, non spiritual origin to BIBLE, HOLY SPIRIT origin.
   Greek mindset – flesh is inherently evil, Hebrew mindset – flesh is potentially good, all is good.
   2Corinth 7:1; Hebrews 14:12; 1Jn 3:3 – even the BA spirit can be corrupted
   Prophesy is the response of the infilling of the spirit, you can't (are unable to) prophesy from the flesh!

7. "We prophesy by faith", however realise that your faith can exceed your anointing. . .

8. Coming out of isolation and finding either your role and acceptance in your church or prophetic community releases you into your calling

OLD TESTAMENT & NEW TESTAMENT PROPHETS – *differences*

There are various differences in operations between the ways OT & NT prophets operate. These basically stem from major contrasts in the different dispensations they both live.

1. The person who lived in the OT did not have the SPIRIT of GOD in them or even upon them unless they were a priest, prophet or king. In the NT we all have the SPIRIT, we are all blessed with the privilege of hearing His Voice.

2. The OT prophet was often called to speak to a rebellious people creating a 'them and us' scenario. The NT prophet is part of the 5 fold ministry of Christ, we are called to serve The Bride of Christ, a people who seek to serve and please GOD.

3. The major ministry of a OT prophet was to speak on behalf of GOD. The major function of a NT prophet is to equip saints to hear GOD for themselves!

4. There was little mandate on the OT prophet to love the people e.g. Jonah. This is the opposite of what is demanded of a NT prophet.
These factors give rise to major differences when it comes to judging prophets as well as the operation and mindsets of prophets.

    Fallibility – In the NT prophet there is room of error, it is expected. This was not allowed in the OT prophet.

The NT prophet must be much more open to being teachable, dependent on The SPIRIT and open to the correction of others.

PROPHETS & church growth – The building of the walls prospered as the prophets prophesied. The prophets encouraged them, keep doing God's will, keep building!

PROPHETIC 'TEST RUNS'

Scripture: Genesis 37; Exodus 2

There are times that seeming confirmations come to you about a project or event and based on these you press ahead with something only to find out later on that it was not actually time for this project. This can be frustrating and cause quite a bit of confusion. These are allowed by The LORD as practice runs for the actual, main event which will come to pas s in due course. Why do these happen? As preparatory ground for future events, but also because, they achieve two more purposes.

1. They prepare you, the vessel that GOD is going to eventually use. These 'dummy runs' are humbling, that's good.
2. They prepare events, people and circumstances around you. If you had not ventured out; though out of timing these circumstances would not have been made ready for the real deal.

PREPARATION

Prophets learn early on to cope with rejection. They learn to depend on GOD in a way that other ministry offices will not find necessary

PROPHETIC COMPANIONS, ROUNDTABLES, COUNCILS

1Samuel 10:5;19:20; Acts 11:27

Prophets seldom walk alone, there is safety in being part of a group

PROPHETS & SOCIAL JUSTICE

Persons that are used to bring social justice are often those whose primary calling is prophetic. Prophetic in the sense that they reflect and speak the heart of GOD for a people and nation.

PROPHETIC CHARACTER –

2Samuel 17:23
Prophetic Maturing, You are a child if you receive a prophecy for someone and your word is not received and acted upon and it makes you depressed. We grow in humility.

Receiving: Sometimes a word can be so obscure and clouded by the style of the vessel that has brought it that it takes great grace to extract any substance from it! Keep trying, if confused ask for help from more mature ones. The 5% degree of truth embedded in it can well be worth the effort.

Giving: Do your best to understand your individual foibles and idiosyncrasies that often inadvertently make the picture of what The SPIRIT has given you cloudy and vague. Recognise these things in your delivery and even offer them as an appendix to the word. For example you may say, 'I hear GOD best in King James English, that's just how HE speaks to me / how my spirit man has been trained to hear HIS Voice.

5 ROLES OF NEW TESTAMENT PROPHETS

1. To teach believers to hear GOD by themselves
2. To help people find and stay in a place of rest and quiet in their hearts
3. To activate spiritual gifts in a church especially prophecy
4. To assist churches to build structure and protocols for the use of prophetic gifts
5. To prophesy to the church, it's leaders and it's people

LESSON 21: PROPHETIC APPOINTMENTS

GUIDELINES

1. Team members should be <u>conversant with the material</u> covered in A PROPHETIC TRAINING eg "what is prophecy?", "weighing prophecy", "using analogies", "prophetic ministry" and "leading break out groups".

2. Unity if key. Commitment to the ministry (in attendance and support) and to building relationally with one another, are essential to forge strong bonds. We are <u>each called to be "a part of"</u> the "quiche being prepared"

3. We have an altar we go to before every session of PROPHETIC APPOINTMENTS. The <u>grace and the unction flow from here.</u>

4. We need not be cast down or feel disqualified by temporary issues which life throws at us ever so often - take them to the altar! <u>GOD can use even our brokenness as we lean on His Grace</u>. There may often be periods of warfare trying to preclude our ability to minister.

5. Let us <u>not neglect our personal altars</u> – this prepares us for growth in prophetic ministry.
    a. Priestly intercession for our loved ones
    b. Worship / soaking (at home, in the car etc)
    c. Word intake (Rhema & Logos)
    d. Praying in the spirit (tongues)
    e. Declarations to shape our world and destiny

6. Our focus is, of course prophetic ministry, but <u>we do not exclude the possibility of</u> pastoral, healing, deliverance stuff etc if it comes up in the session. If more time is needed, schedule another appointment.

7. A <u>leader to each session</u>, supported by at least one other person (room one to "sit in" while learning the ropes.

8. The person sitting in is encouraged to pray along with the others for all heavens counsel to be released.

9. We are for now, not placing any restrictions on type of prophetic word being given – this is <u>to encourage creativity</u>, grow in confidence, step out of comfort zones and get to appreciate one another's gifting.

10. Prophetic words and ministry are to be offered in love and humility. As much as possible use statements like, *"How does this sit with you?*

11. We should <u>weigh the words of others</u> and use statements like: -

    a. *"Yes, that really sits with me too"*
    b. *"I believe this is of GOD, but can we ask GOD to confirm the aspect of .....?"*
    c. *"I felt a slight check in spirit when you said . . . . , can we ask GOD to clarify this area?"*
    d.

12. It is the job of the leader to make sure that the recipient does not leave unsure or confused as to what was and was not said. Much as possible help divide the prophetic words into : -
    a. clear – go for it
    b. put on a shelf and pray about, and
    c. leave this bit out

13. Each session should be recorded and made available to the recipient. A brief report should be written out and filed away.

14. Appointments are <u>10 - 15 minute sessions</u>

    a. Encourage recipients to spend time soaking at the altar "upper room" beforehand
    b. Make the recipient feel relaxed - room temperature / tissues / glass of water (mints for team)
    c. Introduce others present
    d. Assure confidentiality (except they or others are in danger)
    e. Start of the recording with recipient name, time and date of recording
    f. The lead person starts of, others follow (preferably on the same vein to start with)
    g. When praying keep your eyes open – be communicative
    h. Ask for permission before laying on of hands or anointing with oil
    i. Ask the recipient for feed back / questions / clarification
    j. Pray to close the session
    k. Encourage them to spend time again with GOD in the "upper room"

12 TESTS & INDICATORS OF PROPHETIC OFFICE

– developmental stages of "being called" to prophetic office to being "chosen" to being "called, chosen & faithful"
(Matt 20:16; 22:14; Rev 17:14)
(IPAA Guidelines for affirming ministers into
the office of prophet)

A) Calling

1. A testimony of salvation and being filled with The SPIRIT
2. The testament of a calling to the prophetic (Jeremiah 1; Ezek 1; Amos 7; 1Kgs 19)
3. The discovery of a prophetic gift and unction, a seer or nabi; revelational or utterance gift, worship or prayer, fasting or marked levels of supernatural experiences

B) Gift insight & development*

4. Consistent and commensurate gifting (2Corinth 12:12)
5. Endurance and stability (Rev 17:14) having passed the test chosen by GOD which every ministry must undergo (James 1:12)
6. The detection of a particular, prophetic operation and administration (1Corinthians 12:4-6) and/or sphere of influence (2Corinth 10:13)

C) Relationships*

7. Be part of and in good standing in a local church (Hebrews 10:25; Gal 2:2)
8. Having a ministry that is recognised by other leaders in The Body (Gal 2:9)
9. Be linked to an apostle (Eph 2:20, 3:5)

D) Character & Release*

10. A developed character in fulfilment of the conditions for leadership (1Tim3), free from love of money, manipulation or desire to be seen (Is 26:8)

11. A walk of love, humility and accountability to others for both one's personal life as well as fruits of prophetic ministry (Gal 2) as evidenced in an ability to be corrected and to where necessary render an apology

12. Divine release in a *kairos* moment of a GOD given platform (Acts 11:25,26; Titus 1:1-5)

We envisage that an ongoing relationship with the IPAA family offers a forum (not exclusively) for items included in (B), (C) & (D)

NOTES

A prayer to receive JESUS as your LORD and SAVIOUR from sin and it's consequences – separation from GOD and judgement

Dear LORD JESUS,

I believe that you died on the cross for me. I believe that you died in my place for all my sins, all that I have done wrong. I thank You that You loved me enough to give Your life as a sacrifice for mine. I receive your love for me right now; I ask that you take away my sins and all that has been wrong in my life. Please wash me clean and come to live in my heart. I accept you as my LORD and Saviour. Thank you for saving me, for coming into my heart and life. I love you and receive the eternal life that You give right now. Thank You LORD JESUS! Amen.

A prayer to receive the baptism of The HOLY SPIRIT and His gifts

Dear FATHER-GOD,

I thank you for sending JESUS I have received as my LORD and Saviour. Thank You that I now qualify for Your promise to also me to be filled with the power of The HOLY SPIRIT. I come to You on the basis of Your Word, the Bible and right now ask You to fill me, drench me and flood me to overflowing with Your precious gift of the HOLY SPIRIT. HOLY SPIRIT I receive You into my life now in a unique, personal, powerful and special way. Thank You as You fill me, for the gifts You also have to give me especially the divine ability to speak in other tongues and prophecy. I ask for and believe You for these gifts to show up in my life right away! Thank You my FATHER! Thank You LORD JESUS! Thank You precious and dear HOLY SPIRIT! Amen.

Other books by the same author

1. **LEST WE FORGET** – The life and times of the pioneer missionaries to Ibadan, Nigeria (1851 – 1868) As a young girl Anna's dream was to one day be a martyr for JESUS. This is the powerful story of her life along with her husband David, who were the first Christian missionaries to Ibadan in southwest Nigeria from 1851 to 1868. As you read it you will be impacted by a life on fire for GOD!

2. **THE WELLS OF OUR FATHERS** - A history of revival in southwest Nigeria from 1830 to 1959. But this is far more than a history lesson, this is about honouring the lives of all who have gone before us and laid foundations. It is on these foundations that we stand and ascend to the next levels of faith and reformation that The HOLY SPIRIT has in store for us. Life and grace are released as we honour these generals, prophets and apostles who have preceded us. We owe them.

3. **TRANSITION** – Something new is on the horizon! Highlighting areas that The HOLY SPIRIT is revealing to His saints where emphasis and change are needed to break old moulds and be supple to be able to contain the new wine falling on the church. This book starts off with a list of 25 such areas then hones in on six of them including restoration of the prophetic and apostolic offices.

4. **CROSSOVER!** – A manual for transcending societal & cultural obstacles for maximum impact. This book is a reminder of the love The FATHER has for the cultures and nations of the world. Featuring practical ways for social contextulisation including how to conduct socially open church services and contemporary evangelistic paradigms. The FATHER's love is portrayed for us as individuals freeing us to our unique and precious identities.

5. **YOU CAN PROPHESY! 70 truths about the gift of prophecy** - A handy and concise resource covering 22 Reasons to Prophesy, 7 Ways to Prepare for Prophetic Words and Encounters, 7 Ways to Activate Prophetic Grace and loads more. This book presents prophesy as a gift available to every believer, it is not a mark of some great level or height of spirituality.

6. **TRAINING & ACTIVATION MANUALS** – *Equipping the saints (Ephesians 4:11)* - Three resources for training in all righteousness that the man of GOD may be fully equipped in primary areas of the faith. – *Equipping the saints (Ephesians 4:11)*

    a. **25 types of Prayer, Tongues and Interpretation** – all in one manual. LORD teach us to pray was the cry of the disciples, 'LORD make it ours too!'

    b. **Prophecy and Prophetic evangelism** – this gift belongs to us! It is not just for the super saint! Covering all the basics you need to walk in prophecy as your spiritual inheritance.

    c. **Faith, Working Of Miracles & Gifts Of Healings – 21 ways GOD heals today!**

ABOUT THE AUTHOR

Robin, a Nigerian Englishman, runs *Servant Ministries*, an equipping ministry that operates through teaching, preaching, book writing and conferences. He is the convener of the *Inter Prophetic Apostolic Alliance* (IPAA), a coalition of apostolic and prophetic ministers running with a vision to be a voice to the nations and the re-establishment of apostolic structure. He also leads the *Nigeria Academy of Prophetic & Apostolic Reform* (NAPAR).

Robin is passionate to see the church transition to the 'new' that GOD desires to accomplish around the world. In July 1996 Robin received a vision for mission's fires in Nigeria, Africa & Europe. Since then he has been in active pursuit of GOD for a move of the HOLY SPIRIT that will trigger this and other events. In December 1999 in obedience to a divine call he immigrated to the UK as a 'return missionary'.

Robin is the author of "THE BLAZE OF TRANSITION" as well as several manuals on prophetic ministry and books on revival (see amazon.co.uk). His ministry (S.M) is part of "Churches in Communities" led by Dr Hugh Osgood; he is commissioned as a prophet under IPAA as well as "Christian International Europe" (CIE) led by Dr Sharon Stone. He is a spiritual son of Apostle Mosy Madugba (MPN).

Robin releases a monthly "Word for the month" on YouTube ("Robin Jegede-Brimson"). He worships and serves at various churches that he is relationally connected with across London & Kent.

He is an avid squash player and loves spending time in his garden. He is married to Nyema, a worshipper and prophetic intercessor passionate about the ministry of healing. They are blessed with four grown up children and enjoy the grace of GOD living in the seaside town of Whitstable, Kent.

Printed in Great Britain
by Amazon